O

Strategies for Online Learners

A Hacker Handbooks Supplement

Marcy Carbajal Van Horn
St. Edward's University

BEDFORD / ST. MARTIN'S   BOSTON ◆ NEW YORK

Manufactured in the United States of America.

6   5   4   3   2   1
f   e   d   c   b   a

For information, write: Bedford/St. Martin's, 75 Arlington Street, Boston, MA 02116   (617-399-4000)

ISBN-10: 0-312-54370-0
ISBN-13: 978-0-312-54370-9

ACKNOWLEDGMENT

Course screen shots reprinted courtesy of Santa Monica College and Professor Dana Del George.

Strategies for
Online Learners

O Strategies for Online Learners

Online learning presents opportunities to pursue educational goals you might not otherwise be able to fit into your schedule and gives you a chance to take your learning into your own hands. It also gives you a chance to learn to collaborate with others using technology to work, write, communicate, and learn. You can take advantage of these opportunities if you prepare yourself for the online learning environment, find ways to stay motivated, treat other learners with respect, and address challenges with creativity and flexibility.

01 Preparing to learn online

The most successful online learners tend to be committed, engaged, and willing to seek solutions to problems. They take the time to reflect on their own needs and learning styles and to discover more about their online learning environment.

TIP: Before you start your online course, you might want to familiarize yourself with some of the terms that are associated with online learning. When you see an unfamiliar term, either in your course materials or in this book, you can refer to the brief glossary in the back (p. O-37) or to a dictionary. You can also ask your instructor for help.

01-a Check your readiness for online learning.

Before you begin your first online course, take some time to reflect on your needs and preferences to determine whether you are ready to be a successful online learner. Your instructor or school might even provide a self-assessment quiz or questionnaire to help you with this process.

> **My online learning**
>
> "The availability of online courses is a huge benefit to me, since I don't live on campus. I don't have to worry about a long commute multiple times a week, especially on days when I also have to work."
> —Frans Ekendahl, student, Southern New Hampshire University

As the chart on page O-4 shows, those who succeed in online courses are often self-motivated, disciplined, and organized; typically, they are also strong readers and engaged communicators. While successful online students often enjoy the challenges of independent learning, they also enjoy interacting regularly and sharing with their peers. In other words, they don't take courses online as a way to avoid other people.

Take a look at the following chart. How many of these qualities and skills apply to you? Which of these is your real strength? Think about the ways in which your current lifestyle is suited to an online course. What adjustments might you have to make? Finally, do you have the tools you need to succeed in an online course? Take the opportunity to reflect on your readiness for online learning.

Qualities, skills, and tools of successful online learners

Personal qualities

Successful online learners . . .

- are self-motivated and self-directed
- are resourceful and puzzle out solutions to problems
- are comfortable with challenges
- are organized
- have good time management skills
- complete their work with few reminders
- like discussing ideas with others
- can communicate effectively with individuals and groups online

Reading and writing skills

Successful online learners . . .

- have strong reading skills
- are able to follow written directions without also hearing them
- can write clear, concise messages in a timely manner
- feel comfortable sharing feedback about writing

Lifestyle

Successful online learners . . .

- have friends and family who actively support their educational goals
- have enough time to commit to succeeding in an online course
- understand that one course is equivalent to a part-time job and that a full course load is equivalent to a full-time job
- make an effort to balance school, work, and family commitments

Computer skills

Successful online learners . . .

- type quickly
- know how to navigate the Web to find reliable answers to questions
- can easily upload and download documents
- know how to send and receive e-mail—with and without attachments
- know how to use help tools or help menus to find answers to questions about software

Hardware, software, and Internet connection

Successful online learners . . .

- have regular (preferably daily) access to a reliable personal computer
- use an Internet browser and a word processing program that meet their instructor's requirements
- have regular (preferably daily) access to a reliable high-speed Internet connection that supports interactivity and smooth streaming of audio and video files

If you don't yet fit the profile of a successful online learner, think about whether you are willing to adapt your study habits and communication styles in ways that will help you succeed. Because online learning isn't right for everyone, you might realize that a traditional, on-campus class would better suit your needs. In many cases, though, you can set goals, acquire a few skills, and make small behavioral adjustments that will greatly increase your chances of success.

If you're committed to learning online, the strategies and suggestions in this book can help you make the most of your experience.

As you learn

How do you hope to benefit from taking one or more online courses? Describe what motivates you to succeed and how you have prepared yourself for online learning.

01-b Understand the similarities and differences between traditional and online courses.

Traditional and online courses share important similarities. In both situations, instructors and colleges establish learning outcomes,
and students complete tasks and assignments to show that they have achieved those
outcomes. In both types of courses, students
are expected to read course materials, participate in discussions, complete writing assignments, and perhaps take tests or complete
other assessments. The primary difference
between online and traditional courses is *how*
information is communicated.

While students and instructors in most
traditional classes interact with both spoken
and written communication, students and instructors in online courses
typically interact through written communication: posted lectures,
downloadable presentations, and typed discussion posts. This communication is usually asynchronous — that is, the participants are not online
at the same time. For example, you might be referring to material that
your instructor posted at the beginning of the course or responding to
discussion posts that a classmate wrote the previous day. When synchronous (or real-time) activities, such as chat-based meetings, are built
into an online course, some form of written communication is usually
involved. The chart on pages O-7 to O-8 describes some of the activities
that are common to both traditional and online writing courses. Notice
their similarities as well as their differences.

> **My online learning**
>
> "What really surprises me
> is that taking an online
> course is far harder than
> taking a regular in-class
> course. I thought that it
> would be a breeze to take
> an online course, but it
> is the opposite. I came
> to like it because of the
> flexibility—and the fact
> that I'm never stuck in
> traffic getting to class."
> —Glennard Tiu, student,
> Santa Monica College

> **As you learn**
>
> Take a few minutes to reflect on the lists of activities that are typical in on-
> line and traditional courses (see pp. O-7 to O-8). In your online course, have
> you found the activities more like or less like the activities you have experi-
> enced in traditional courses? What surprises you about either the similarities
> or the differences between the two kinds of courses?

Typical activities in traditional and online writing courses

	Traditional (on-campus) courses	Online courses
LECTURES	▪ Instructors deliver lectures in person, in front of a group of students, at a specific time. Although a slide show presentation can be viewed again if the instructor makes it available, the lecture itself—as an event—can't be re-created.	▪ Instructors post information in the form of Web pages (on the course platform), attached documents, slide show presentations, or other media. Often students can view or listen to course lectures at their convenience. Unless instructors close completed course units, students can review these materials at any point during the semester.
DISCUSSIONS	▪ In most class sessions, only a few students speak while other students listen. Students might be expected to facilitate discussions during the semester. Each discussion is a one-time event; the exact situation and content can't be re-created at a later date.	▪ Typically, all students are required to contribute to every online discussion and read their peers' comments. Students might be expected to facilitate discussions during the semester. Even though the discussion might end on a particular date, students can typically review messages throughout the semester.
ESSAY ASSIGNMENTS	▪ Writing assignments often follow a process approach: Students might be required to complete prewriting, revision, and editing activities during class or at home.	▪ Writing assignments often follow a process approach: Students might be required to complete prewriting, revision, and editing activities online or offline.

→

Typical activities in traditional and online writing courses (continued)

	Traditional (on-campus) courses	Online courses
PEER REVIEW	▪ Students typically exchange drafts and comment on peers' essays according to set criteria. Although a few comments might be written, students usually discuss comments face-to-face.	▪ Students e-mail or post essay drafts for other students to review. The discussion among peers often takes the form of typed comments on a paper or posts to a discussion board.
QUIZZES, TESTS, AND SIMILAR ASSESSMENTS	▪ Although quiz items might be read out loud, quizzes and tests are typically completed on paper in class; questions might be in multiple-choice, short-answer, or essay format. The time limit for quizzes and tests is usually rigid.	▪ Quizzes and tests are typically completed online using quiz tools that are part of the course platform; questions might be in multiple-choice, short-answer, or essay format. The time limit might be rigid or flexible. Self-assessments that are designed with the quiz tool might not be graded or might be assigned points on a credit/no-credit basis.
CONFERENCES	▪ Conferences are typically face-to-face and take place in class, in the instructor's office on campus, or at another campus location.	▪ Instructors might conduct conferences with their students by e-mail, by phone, or in a chat room. If students live nearby, instructors might ask students to come to the campus for a face-to-face meeting.

While an online format can make your course more convenient and accessible, it won't necessarily make your course easier. In fact, because students are responsible for reading, digesting, and reviewing course content on their own time and for typing thoughtful messages instead of listening and talking in class, the total time spent completing an online course might actually be greater than the total time spent completing a traditional, on-campus course. With the chart below as a guide, check your own assumptions against the realities of online learning, and adjust your schedule or behaviors as needed. You might also want to seek advice or feedback from a student who has completed an online course.

Faulty assumptions versus the realities of online learning

Faulty assumption	Reality
• The online course will be easier than its on-campus equivalent.	• Although the delivery method is different, the course content and essay assignments will be similar to those in the course's on-campus equivalent.
• The online course will take less time than its on-campus equivalent.	• Because most of the communication is written rather than spoken (and because it takes most people longer to type than to speak), you'll probably spend *more* rather than less time completing an online course. Use your school's formula for estimating the time you will need for your online course. As a general rule, you should expect to spend three to five hours per week, per course credit, completing work for a semester-length course. This means that a three-credit, semester-length course will require about nine to fifteen hours of your time each week. Accelerated courses might require twenty or more hours of your time each week.

→

Faulty assumptions versus the realities of online learning (continued)

Faulty assumption

- The online course schedule is completely flexible; you can complete assignments at any time.

- Because all of the content is online all the time, you can pick and choose the order in which you complete assignments.

- Group projects aren't assigned in online courses. Because students don't sit in class together, all work is completed independently.

- You won't need your own computer or Internet connection to complete an online course—just access to a computer lab.

Reality

- Most online courses follow a strict schedule. The instructor will probably designate set due dates for discussion posts, essay drafts, peer review posts, quizzes, and other assignments. While you can often read material or complete the assignments at any time *before* the due dates, you typically can't post content *after* a due date has passed.

- Most online course assignments follow a specific order; you'll probably have to complete several steps in sequence to complete longer assignments. Some instructors might restrict access to certain information until you have completed preliminary steps. (Check your syllabus for specific information.)

- Discussions and group work are common components of online courses. For most courses, you should expect to communicate with your instructor and your peers on a regular basis throughout the semester. You might even be required to complete a group paper or project.

- Most students who attempt to complete an online course without their own computer or Internet connection have difficulties managing their time effectively. Because the computer lab might be closed or crowded when you need to be online, it is best to have your own reliable equipment and reliable Internet access.

02 Becoming familiar with your online course

Part of your preparation will involve familiarizing yourself with both the course platform and the class materials. Before you begin the course—or as soon as possible after you have begun—take some time to browse through the course platform features and contents so that you can work confidently throughout the semester.

02-a Learn to navigate the course platform and other technology.

A course platform is a software program—such as eCollege, Blackboard, Desire2Learn, or Moodle—that your college and instructor use to deliver course materials to you. Although each system has its own interface and design, most platforms have similar basic components that instructors use to communicate with their students. The exact tools and the way they are used may vary, depending on the instructor's preference and the purpose of the course, but the following are the most common:

- a home or welcome page for the course
- content units or folders
- an assignments hub or page
- a discussion forum
- an instant-messaging tool (like a chat room)
- an e-mail tool

> **As you learn**
>
> Which course platform is your instructor or school using to deliver the course? Identify the components and tools available in your course. Make a note: How can you access tutorials that explain how to make the most of the course components and tools?

Early on in the course—or before it begins, if possible—take some time to navigate the course platform. Look through the components; try out any tutorials that are offered by your school or as part of the platform. If you don't understand how to use the tools or components, click the help link on the course's main page or visit the help section of the platform's Web site. There you will see detailed descriptions and instructions for contacting the appropriate technical support office. (For additional tips, see O5-a and O5-b.) The following discussion, which illustrates some of the most commonly used online course components, can help you get started.

Commonly used online course components and tools

Course platforms are analogous to traditional classrooms: Just as a traditional classroom has tools for class discussion and activities (for example, a chalkboard or whiteboard, a projection system, and a podium for instructors), an online classroom also has tools for communication and presentation. This section illustrates some of the components most commonly used in online writing courses; however, the exact tools and the way they are used may vary, depending on the instructor's preference and the purpose of the course.

HOME PAGE OR WELCOME PAGE FOR THE COURSE   The course home page often includes a welcome message, your instructor's contact information, and links to the other course components. Check the welcome page regularly to see updates and announcements from your instructor.

Home pages sometimes show who else in your class is online at a given time. Knowing who is online can be very helpful if you are stuck on a problem or unclear about an assignment or due date. You can often chat with other students who are online and help each other with assignments.

HOME PAGE FOR ENGLISH COMPOSITION I

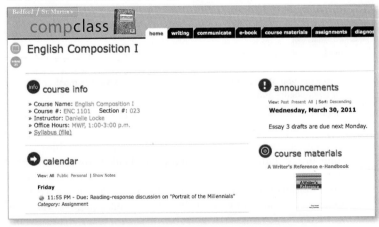

COURSE CONTENT UNITS   Content units—sometimes called *modules, categories, instructor-added materials,* or *chapters*—contain materials for study and discussion. In most cases, a main menu or a table of contents will direct you to the different units available in your course. Each unit will probably have its own menu of tasks, documents, and presentations. Some courses might have one unit for each week; other courses might have one unit for each major topic covered.

The illustration below shows an introductory page for a content unit on narrowing a topic. A menu on the left hand side of the page directs students to assignments and activities.

INTRODUCTORY PAGE FOR A CONTENT UNIT

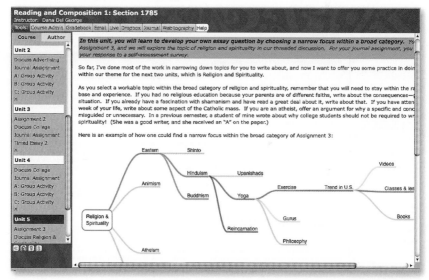

ASSIGNMENTS The assignments page typically provides links to major assignments, such as essays and final projects. Pay attention to the due date for each assignment; the link might become unavailable once the due date has passed. Your instructor might require additional assignments—such as readings, discussion postings, or peer reviews—that are not listed on the assignments page. Check your syllabus for specific details. (See also 02-b.)

The assignment shown in the illustration below, a peer review workshop assignment, requires students to attach a draft of their own and review two classmates' drafts by the end of the week.

PEER REVIEW ASSIGNMENT

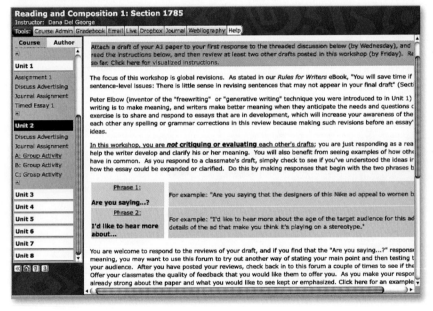

DISCUSSION FORUMS (ASYNCHRONOUS COMMUNICATION) Discussion forums—also called *discussion boards* or *threaded discussions*—are pages that allow multiple students to post messages on a specific topic. In most cases, all students in the course can read these messages. Discussion forums are used for asynchronous communication; students do not have to be logged on to the discussion board at the same time as their classmates to post or read comments. Class discussions help students understand what is expected on assignments, and they help everyone understand the readings and other resources for the course.

If you are expected to contribute to a discussion forum, you are being asked to make serious, thoughtful, well-considered posts that will be shared with everyone in the class. It's like raising your hand in class. When you participate in a discussion, you want to show that you are prepared, that you have thought through the question, and that you have something useful to contribute. (See the chart on p. O-30 for tips on participating in asynchronous discussions.)

LIST OF DISCUSSION FORUMS

CHAT ROOMS, LIVE CHAT, AND INSTANT MESSAGING (SYNCHRONOUS COMMUNICATION) Chat rooms or similar tools are used for synchronous (real-time) communication. Two or more users are logged on to the class at the same time and take turns posting and replying to messages. If you use personal chat or social networking posts to stay in touch with friends, you may be accustomed to exchanging sly or funny remarks. Such behavior is fun during personal chats but inappropriate in a class setting.

Monitor your chat contributions and work to be constructive and to keep a useful chat moving along. Think about your instructor's purpose for holding a chat session, and then see if you can be a constructive contributor. Remember that you are building an identity and reputation during these chat sessions, and you want to be well regarded by others. (See the chart on p. O-31 for tips on participating in synchronous discussions.)

LIVE CHAT AMONG MEMBERS OF A PEER REVIEW GROUP

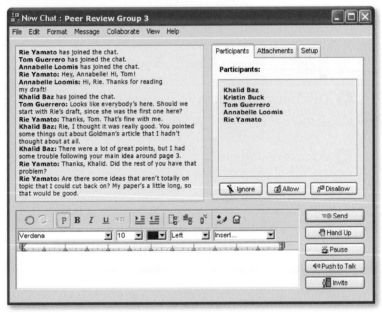

COURSE E-MAIL (PERSONAL COMMUNICATION)   The course e-mail tool is separate from your personal e-mail account and allows you to send personal messages to your instructor and peers within the course platform. No e-mail address is required. Only the recipient—not the entire class—can see these messages. Because communication is carried out inside the class platform, you need to be sure to check that e-mail frequently. Otherwise you might miss helpful messages, changes to assignments or due dates, or advice on being prepared for class.

PRIVATE E-MAIL MESSAGE FROM A COURSE PARTICIPANT

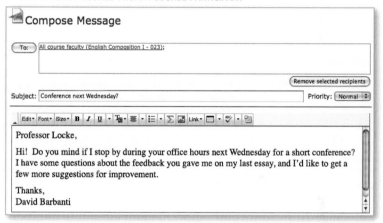

OTHER TOOLS   Depending on your context and instructor, you might also be required to use tools outside of the course platform. For example, instructors often use blogs (Weblogs) and wikis for collaborative writing or sharing. Your instructor will probably provide specific instructions for using such technology for your course; however, if you need additional help or information, use the blog's or wiki's help features or ask your instructor for further guidance.

02-b Become familiar with the course materials and requirements.

Unlike the course tools, the course content is specific to your instructor and college. Although some of the course materials (such as the exercises in CompClass) might be commercially produced, most of them have probably been created by your instructor. Each instructor has a different style, so no two courses will look exactly the same, even if the same course platform is used. To find out the specific requirements for your course, read through the materials carefully. Pay particular attention to the syllabus, special announcements, and content pages, and try to discern logical patterns in the course materials.

Syllabus

Typically, the syllabus provides basic information about your course—including the description, outcomes and objectives, specific requirements for passing the course, and your instructor's contact information. One of the first steps to taking an online course, or any course for that matter, is to read the syllabus carefully. After you read it the first time, make a copy of it that you can access offline—especially for times when you can't be online for technical or other reasons.

When you read the syllabus, pay particular attention to special requirements for online attendance and participation. In addition, make note of your instructor's policies regarding server problems, power outages caused by inclement weather, and other computer-related issues. Your instructor probably has a specific policy in place so that you can avoid too many disruptions in course work when special circumstances arise. When you encounter difficulties, notify your instructor as soon as possible.

As you learn

Take a careful look at the syllabus for your course. How will your instructor measure attendance and participation? What recommendations does your instructor give for dealing with computer issues? Does the syllabus provide more than one way to contact your instructor? Review the syllabus for any information that seems unclear, and check in with your instructor for clarification.

Announcements

Instructors often post updates or other time-sensitive messages on the course home page or on calendars. Your instructor will typically let you know at the beginning of the course which method he or she will use to communicate updates to you. You should check the designated announcements area regularly or you might miss important information or notices of changes. The reminders or updates posted there are similar to the information instructors give at the end or beginning of class to on-site students.

> **My online learning**
>
> "I found that I had to make sure to schedule certain hours of the day to focus on my assignments. That helped."
>
> —Shannon Cohn, student, Santa Monica College

Content pages

Similar to lectures that an on-site instructor would give, content pages (all of the pages inside the content units) typically provide the substance of the course. They might include presentations about course content, instructions for completing assignments, or instructions for interacting with your classmates. To learn the course material and complete assignments successfully, you will need to read these pages carefully.

Logical patterns

Lessons and instructional units will probably follow a specific pattern, no matter what tools your instructor uses to communicate information about the course. You might find, for example, that each content unit begins with an introduction, presents the body of information under headings, and ends with a conclusion that tells students what steps to take next. You might also find that your instructor follows a set pattern of tasks for each major unit of instruction: for example, *one reading, a quiz, a discussion, and then an essay assignment*; or *two readings, a discussion, and then an essay assignment*. If you can, take some time to browse through the course materials to discover these patterns. Knowing what to expect will help you plan your time, monitor your own learning and progress, and find clarification when necessary.

03 Participating actively in online courses

Successful online learners engage actively with their course materials, instructor, and peers. Create success for yourself by managing your time and communicating regularly with those in your online learning community.

03-a Set priorities and manage your time effectively.

Online classes require that you manage your time wisely. Because the course is accessible twenty-four hours a day, seven days a week, you might be tempted to procrastinate, telling yourself that the material "will be there tomorrow." By contrast, if you're a first-time online learner and are especially nervous about missing some information, you might become obsessive about logging on to your course several times a day when only one check-in is necessary.

One of the best ways to avoid either of these extremes is to create a schedule. As you might with other courses, you can use a personal calendar or planner to mark due dates and establish a plan for completing assignments. Referring to the syllabus or the calendar that your instructor provides, first record the course due dates for major assignments, such as essays, projects, or term papers. Next, add the due dates for shorter assignments that you need to submit, such as discussion posts, essay drafts, and peer reviews. Finally, with your personal and other academic commitments in mind, set your own *personal* due dates for these assignments and the smaller steps you need to take to complete them. Your personal due dates might fall on or before the actual course due dates, depending on your obligations. For example, if Wednesday is the due date for a particular discussion post but you have to take your son to soccer practice every Wednesday afternoon, make Monday or Tuesday night your personal due date—ahead of schedule.

> **My online learning**
>
> "Contrary to what I had expected, the online class forum is a more thought-provoking environment. It demands more carefully thought out responses to the course work than I was ever able to produce in a classroom."
> —Natalie Kok, student, Regent University

Once you've established a semester plan, transfer the information to weekly or daily to-do lists so that you can keep up-to-date with all course requirements.

TIP: Check both the due *dates* and the *times* very carefully. Many course platforms allow instructors to close assignments at particular times—noon or midnight, for example—on the due dates. Carefully read the assignment information so that you do not miss the deadline. Because assignment settings might be automated by the software system, minutes—and sometimes even seconds—may make the difference between being able to turn in an assignment or not. If you live far from your school, pay attention to possible time-zone differences.

DUE DATE AND TIME FOR AN ASSIGNMENT

> **Friday**
>
> 🌑 11:55 PM - Due: Reading-response discussion
> *Category:* Assignment

Give the course—and yourself—a chance. Every new experience has its own learning curve, and you might feel a little overwhelmed when you start your first online course. Your progress might be slower at the beginning of the semester, while you are still learning how to navigate the course platform and tools, so make additional room in your schedule as necessary. As you gain confidence with the software, you will be able to navigate through the course more quickly and to devote most, if not all, of your study time to the course content itself.

As you learn

For an upcoming assignment, develop a personal planner similar to the one that appears on page O-22. Be sure to balance time needed for all parts of the assignment—including reading, research, or feedback—with time needed for personal commitments or job-related commitments.

Using the course calendar and a personal planner to manage your time

Below are two sample calendars: a course calendar, with due dates set by the instructor to fall on Wednesdays and Fridays; and a student's personal planner. The student has written and highlighted the course due dates on her planner but has set personal goals to complete the assignments *before* the course due dates. These personal goals will help her complete the assignments without rushing to finish at the last minute.

ASSIGNMENT CALENDAR WITH DUE DATES

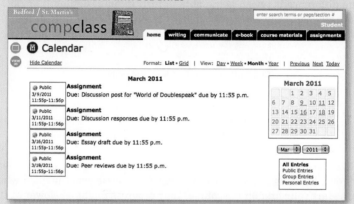

PERSONAL PLANNER—MARCH 2011

SUNDAY	MONDAY	TUESDAY	WEDNESDAY	THURSDAY	FRIDAY	SATURDAY
6	**7**	**8**	**9**	**10**	**11**	**12**
Read "World of Doublespeak" and preview the discussion questions	Write and post discussion responses online		Discussion post due	Read classmates' posts and respond to three ✳✳ First review the directions for the upcoming essay assignment	Response due	
13	**14**	**15**	**16**	**17**	**18**	**19**
Plan essay and write a rough draft	Revise the draft and post it to the peer review page	Finish essay draft today	(Dentist appointment) Essay draft due	Read two classmates' papers and post peer reviews	Peer reviews due	

03-b Communicate regularly with your instructor and classmates.

Just as you would in an on-site course, pay attention to your instructor's attendance requirements, which you should be able to find in the syllabus. Although you might not be required to visit the physical campus, your instructor probably can determine whether you have visited the course site and viewed the course materials regularly. Some instructors track page hits (the number of times you visit each page in the course) or the number of minutes you spend viewing each unit; other instructors require that you complete assignments to show your continued attendance. Most courses require a certain number of check-ins each week. Be sure to follow your instructor's guidelines and to set regular check-in times on your personal calendar.

> **My online learning**
>
> "The most surprising part of the online class has been the help and support of my fellow classmates and my instructor. I figured I would be on my own, since it's just me and my laptop. But I was pleasantly surprised to have help from the entire class."
> —Kamehalani Ortiz, student, Honolulu Community College

In courses that require a significant amount of interaction, you might have to communicate in some way—either by posting to the discussion board, by reviewing a peer's draft, or by completing a quiz—to show that you have "attended" the class for the week. If you visit the course site but do not communicate through the means your instructor requires, you might be counted absent. In some contexts, too many absences (or missed assignments) might result in your being blocked or dropped from the course. Check your syllabus carefully for your instructor's specific policies.

In courses that depend heavily on discussion and peer review, be sure that you participate and submit your work promptly. Doing so demonstrates respect for your peers. In some cases, your peers might not be able to complete their assigned work (such as peer reviews or responses to discussion posts) until you have completed yours.

Remember, too, that you should contact your instructor whenever you need help understanding the course materials or requirements. In an online course, your instructor can't see facial expressions showing that you might be worried or confused. If you have questions about the course, don't hesitate to communicate with your instructor—by e-mail, by phone, or, if possible, in a face-to-face visit during his or her office hours. (See O5-b for additional tips on getting help with course materials.)

03-c Make adjustments to increase your motivation and participation.

If your level of participation begins to wane because the online format doesn't suit your natural preference for face-to-face learning, try adjusting your habits to increase your motivation. Small behavioral adjustments — such as those listed in the chart below — can help you feel more involved in your class and attentive to your work.

> **As you learn**
>
> How do you motivate yourself to complete coursework? What rituals or practices do you follow when "going to class"?

Tips for increasing motivation

- **Make a friend or two.** Many classes have an open discussion area where students can post messages that are unrelated to the course materials. Use the open discussion area to get to know other students in your class and to build a greater sense of community.

- **Meet the instructor.** You might be close enough to campus to meet your instructor during office hours. Do so if you can. Establishing a face-to-face relationship can increase your sense of responsibility and encourage a sense of partnership with your instructor.

- **Get out of the house.** If you don't like studying alone, try completing your work in a computer lab, where other students will be working online. If you live near your school, form study groups with other students in your course so that you can see your peers face-to-face.

- **Dress the part.** Get ready to study online as you would get ready for a job. Shower, get dressed, and "go to class" — even if the class is just a small office space in the corner of your bedroom. If possible, close the door and ask your friends and family not to disturb you while you are working.

- **Make a contribution.** Contribute some ideas from your independent reading. Or share a handy source or reference work or Web site with your classmates. Making a positive contribution — being generous with ideas and information — increases your sense of worth and involvement in your class.

- **Tune in to your body clock.** Work on your course materials when you are most alert. If you're a morning person, complete the course materials early, before you go to work or before members of your household wake up. If you prefer staying up late, save your work for the evening hours.

- **Plan ahead.** Preview what is coming. Scanning upcoming readings and assignments can help you feel in control. Finishing an assignment before it is due makes the course and your other obligations seem manageable.

- **Reward yourself.** Set up a simple reward system for yourself as you progress through your course. For example, you can postpone watching your favorite TV show until after you've completed your homework for the week, or you can treat yourself to a movie after you've completed a major project. Create incentives that are meaningful to you.
- **Work offline.** Even though the course materials are delivered online, not all of your work has to be completed on the computer. Reduce eye strain by handwriting some activities—such as brainstorming for an essay or creating an outline.

04 Contributing appropriate content in online courses

If you participate fully, you will probably write more in your online composition class than you will in most other on-site or online courses. Consider each assignment—large or small—an opportunity to grow as a writer by using an appropriate level of clarity, detail, and professionalism.

04-a As you would in any other class, submit your best work.

Because you can't rely on using nonverbal communication (gestures or facial expressions) in online classes, clear written communication is especially important. Remember, too, that online classes aren't less professional than on-site classes. They have similar objectives, and they require just as much effort. Don't take your assignments less seriously simply because they are online.

In this age of hypermedia, texting, and online social networking, it might be tempting to use shorthand or very casual language in your online classes. At best, these forms might appear comical; at worst, they might be confusing, annoying, or even offensive to others. While it's perfectly acceptable to use shorthand language in informal contexts, you should use formal academic English for your course work and course communication—including e-mail and discussion posts. Your grasp of academic English might not be perfect, but you should at least try to use clear language that is both friendly and professional in tone. Doing so will ensure that other readers understand your intended meaning and are not confused or offended by your work.

Shortcuts to avoid in online classes

ALL CAPITAL LETTERS	Some people try to save time and eliminate typos by writing with the caps lock key engaged. However, using all capital letters can make your writing appear angry or offensive.
ALL LOWERCASE LETTERS	Like sentences in all capital letters, sentences that are written with only lowercase letters can be difficult for readers to process. These sentences can also give the impression that the writer is not taking readers or the assignment seriously.
TEXTING LANGUAGE	Short forms like *b4* for *before* or *IMO* for *in my opinion* might confuse readers who aren't familiar with them. These forms are too casual for course discussions and assignments.
OMITTED PUNCTUATION	Sentences that lack punctuation are difficult to understand. Even if your punctuation isn't perfect, you should at least attempt to use standard conventions.

04-b Communicate courteously and professionally with your instructor and classmates.

In addition to writing formally, use common sense and courtesy when communicating in your online classroom, and avoid writing anything that you wouldn't say in a face-to-face setting. See the chart on page O-27 for examples of appropriate comments.

> **My online learning**
>
> "In my course's online chat room, classmates interact with each other more openly and honestly than in discussions in an on-campus classroom."
> —Caroline Knab, student, Santa Monica College

Dealing with controversial topics

Much of the content in college courses is meant to push you to think critically—often in ways that can challenge your assumptions or preconceptions. When discussing controversial topics, you might find that you disagree with your peers. It's appropriate to hold different views, but you should be respectful when expressing your disagreement. Be logical and fair, and don't attack your classmates personally.

Communicating courteously and professionally with peers

Using the right tone

Inappropriate	Appropriate
■ You're so wrong.	■ I can see your point, but I disagree because . . .
■ That chick doesn't know what she's talking about. It's stupid to think that war is like a disease.	■ I disagree with the author's view that war is like a disease. Although I understand her argument, I feel that she could have used more convincing support.

Offering sound advice

Inappropriate	Appropriate
■ Awkward.	■ I'm not sure what you're trying to say here. You might want to clarify this sentence by . . .
■ I don't understand this paper at all. You don't make any sense.	■ I was confused by the main points in your paper. You might want to reread the assignment or ask the instructor for help.

Eliminating confusing slang, idioms, and jargon

Inappropriate	Appropriate
■ Sup?	■ What's up? How are you doing?
■ You shouldn't look a gift horse in the mouth.	■ If someone offers you helpful advice, you should be grateful, not critical.
■ IMHO, you need to back this up more.	■ Can you provide more evidence to support your point?

Offering sound advice in peer reviews

Similarly, when conducting peer reviews, help your classmates with constructive advice, not harsh criticism. In your review, try to point out at least one or two of the paper's strengths. If you point out a weakness, accompany your feedback with a polite suggestion for improvement. Instead of writing short, choppy phrases that could be misinterpreted, write complete sentences that convey your desire to help your peer improve.

Writing with diversity in mind

When you can't see or hear your classmates in person, it's sometimes easy to forget that they come from a variety of backgrounds and may have differing levels of experience. Keep in mind that there will probably be a mix of genders, ages, cultural contexts, and linguistic backgrounds in your online community. Eliminate any sexist language from your online communication, and—out of respect for those who might not understand it—try to avoid using obscure slang, highly idiomatic language, or jargon. See the sections on word choice in your handbook.

Writing with longevity and portability in mind

Remember that what is on the Web is public and portable: It can be copied, pasted, and sent to other students, teachers, and individuals outside your school. As a general rule, write only comments that you wouldn't mind sharing with the instructor or the rest of the class. In addition, be respectful and do not copy and paste anyone else's comments to other forms of media. Keep class communication within the course itself.

Reading with an open mind

When you're reading messages from your instructor or peers, try to assume that the writer's tone is neutral. Assume that each person is communicating with the best of intentions, and avoid taking offense at messages that seem too direct. If your classmate or instructor asks a question, read it as an inquiry rather than as a personal challenge or probe.

04-c Use the appropriate level of detail and clarity in asynchronous and synchronous discussions.

Discussions in an online class might take place in discussion forums, which allow students to log on and post at different times (asynchronous), or in chat rooms or similar settings, which require that all participants be logged on at the same time (synchronous).

When communicating in these settings, realize that the purposes of each are slightly different. Asynchronous discussion forums provide an outlet for deeper-level thinking expressed in longer chunks—several sentences and even full paragraphs. Chat-based discussions take place in real time, so messages should be kept shorter—perhaps two or three lines. In both settings, your role as a learner and participant is to advance the discussion and contribute in a meaningful way. The charts on pages O-30 to O-31 can help you make the most of these two types of discussion.

DISCUSSION BOARD

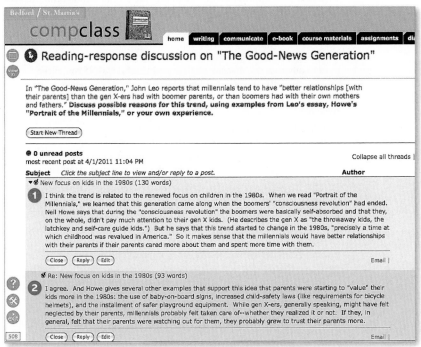

1   The writer of the first post includes detail and stays on topic.

2   The writer of the second post extends the ideas in the first post and takes the conversation a step further.

Tips for participating in asynchronous discussions

The following tips will help you participate productively in discussion forums, discussion boards, and threaded discussions.

- **Read other entries before posting.** You might need to scroll to the bottom of the page to see new messages, or you might need to click the title to expand the comments.

- **Pay attention to how your post fits the discussion.** Are you replying to a particular individual or responding to a particular question? Are you contributing to an existing thread or starting a new one? You want your post to fit in the right place.

- **Title your post appropriately.** Try to provide a brief but meaningful label for what the message contains. Check for specific requirements. Some instructors require that post titles include particular words or elements.

- **Keep the discussion going.** When you respond to a post, be sure to advance the discussion in a meaningful way. If you agree or disagree with the original post, explain why. If you ask a question, try to ask one that calls for more than a one-word response.

- **Use detail.** Avoid posting short comments (like "Good job!" or "Ditto") that don't add substance to the discussion or invite responses. When agreeing with or praising another classmate's comment, explain in detail what you like about the comment.

- **Help your readers understand your ideas.** To provide appropriate context, you may need to start your post by copying and pasting a relevant section of someone else's post. (Be sure to identify the author of the original post.) Take the time to give all readers the information they need to understand your posts.

- **Stay on topic.** As much as possible, stick to the topic of the discussion. If you want to take the conversation in a different direction, give your post a new title so that other students will know you have changed topics.

- **Proofread before posting.** To avoid confusing your readers, write complete ideas in complete sentences without errors. Carefully proofread your message before you post it for the class.

- **Post only what you want the whole class to see.** Save personal messages for e-mail. Remember that discussion boards are public and available to the whole class. As with all of your classroom communication, use courtesy and respect.

Tips for participating in synchronous discussions

The following tips will help you participate productively in chat rooms, instant messaging, and other real-time discussions.

- **Write short messages; divide longer messages into chunks.** To avoid stalling the discussion while you type, limit the amount of information you include in one message. If you have a lot to say, post your idea in chunks of no more than two or three lines per instant message. If your thought is not yet complete, end the chunk with an ellipsis mark (. . .) so that your peers know that you still have more to write. If a peer ends a comment with an ellipsis mark, wait until he or she has finished before you start a new thought.

- **Connect your contributions to the class.** Refer to prior comments from other students and extend the thinking of your classmates. Make connections to lectures, handouts, or other class materials. Show that you can place your comments into the relevant class context.

- **Clarify only when necessary.** Although you should always try to express your ideas clearly, don't worry if one of your posts contains a minor typo. Send corrections of previous messages only when you think you might be misunderstood or when peers ask you for clarification. Sending messages that simply correct typos in previous messages can waste valuable discussion time.

- **Stay on topic.** As much as possible, stick to the topic of the discussion. Do not add off-topic comments to the main discussion; if someone else offers a tangential comment, avoid responding to it. Creating off-topic discussions may frustrate your peers and make them feel that you are wasting their valuable time. While your peers can ignore tangential discussions that form on discussion boards, they can't ignore them in chat rooms.

- **Take turns.** Try to give all participants the opportunity to chat. Avoid monopolizing the discussion. If you've made several separate comments in a row, step back for a bit and give other students an opportunity to share. If you're in doubt about the level of participation expected, see the guidelines your instructor has provided.

As you learn

Reflect on your instructor's expectations for asynchronous and synchronous communication with peers. Are a certain number of posts expected in a week? Are any posts graded? How would you evaluate your participation in the "conversation" of the course so far?

04-d Submit only your own work; avoid copying and pasting from outside sources.

It may seem obvious that students should submit their own work; however, in online classes, the temptation to copy and paste text from outside sources can be greater than it is in on-site classes. Make sure that all of the work you submit—from discussion posts to final essay drafts—is your own. Check your syllabus to make sure you understand your school's academic integrity policies and to learn about the penalties for cheating and plagiarism. See the section on avoiding plagiarism in your handbook.

Also check your own academic practices; you might see opportunities for change. Some writers who plagiarize do so because they feel they don't have enough time to complete the assignment; copying and pasting from another source seems like an easy fix. Planning ahead and managing commitments (see section O-3a) will help you stay in control and make time for your writing. Sometimes writers plagiarize because they feel as if they have nothing of value to say—no interesting or impressive contribution to make. Meeting with your instructor or a peer to talk through your ideas can help. Contributing to the class discussion board or chat is another opportunity for feedback. When you really dive into a discussion, you'll find that others are interested in what you have to say. See the charts on pages O-30 and O-31 for tips on participating actively in class discussions.

> **As you learn**
>
> If a classmate asked you to define plagiarism, how would you respond? If your instructor or school has a plagiarism policy, briefly describe the penalties for plagiarizing someone else's work. What strategies do you use to avoid plagiarism?

≡ 05 Finding extra help

When you take your first online course, you will need to learn how to use the course platform. Picking up the skills of online learning at the same time that you're trying to grasp the course material can feel overwhelming unless you know where to find help. If you need help in updating your computer skills, using the course platform, or understanding the course materials, seek out resources that can help you succeed.

05-a Attend workshops or visit the computer lab to update your computer skills.

Many students say that the greatest challenge involved in taking an online course is simply learning how to use the necessary technology. You don't need to be a computer software expert to take an online course, but you do need a few critical computer skills to be a successful online learner. If you do not yet know how to upload and download documents, navigate the Web, post to a discussion forum, or use a basic word processing program (like Microsoft Word), now is the time to learn. Your school might offer basic computer competency workshops or online readiness tutorials. If no workshops are available, try visiting your school's computer lab; in all likelihood, someone in the lab can teach you how to perform these basic tasks.

05-b For help with your course platform, use help menus or contact technical support.

If you need help with the technology used to deliver your online course materials, use the help menu within the course platform. First, click the help link, which is usually located in the upper right corner of the screen or in the main course menu. Then, a help page will appear, giving you a variety of options for getting assistance, such as tutorials, handouts, and toll-free technical support phone numbers.

CONTACT INFORMATION FOR TECHNICAL SUPPORT

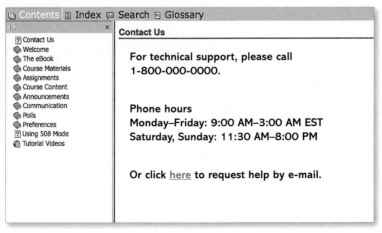

It's a good idea to try out any tutorials or videos designed to help you use the course platform effectively.

If you can't get the help you need by using the tools available on the course platform, your school's distance education office or educational technology office might be able to offer assistance. Most offices have staff available during regular business hours to answer students' questions, and some even offer special workshops or tutorials to help students with common concerns.

If you exhaust these resources and still can't find the help you need, you can ask your instructor for guidance. Remember, however, that your instructor's responsibility is to teach in his or her area of expertise—English composition or literature, for example—not to teach you how to use your computer.

05-c Ask your instructor and peers for help with course materials.

If you don't understand course material—lectures, presentations, handouts, documents, readings, assignments, or directions that your instructor has provided—first reread the material thoroughly and carefully, and follow any tips that are included. If you still need help, contact your instructor directly, either by e-mail or by phone, or, if you live near your school, visit your instructor on campus during office hours. Some instructors set aside online office hours for communicating with their online students. Check your syllabus for your instructor's availability and preferred method of communication.

If you're working at a time when your instructor does not have office hours (late at night, for example), you can also try contacting your peers for help. When you log on to your course platform, you might be able to see who else from your class is online and available to chat. It is a good idea to make a few contacts right at the beginning of the semester. If possible, exchange phone numbers and personal e-mail addresses with other students in your class so that you can ask them for help. Additionally, check your course's discussion forum for a help area. Some instructors set up special discussion threads for peer-to-peer assistance.

05-d For additional feedback on your writing, visit your school's writing center—on campus or online.

If you would like feedback on your writing beyond the peer review offered in your course, consider visiting your school's writing center. If you live close to your campus, make an effort to visit the center in person. If you can't go to the campus for an appointment with a writing tutor, find out whether the writing center offers any online assistance. Some schools have online writing labs (OWLs) with staff specifically trained to meet the needs of online learners. Visit your school's Web site for information.

A brief glossary of online learning terminology

asynchronous Not occurring at the same time. When students participate in asynchronous discussions, they log on at different times to post and read comments. E-mail and messages in discussion forums (including discussion boards and threaded discussions) are forms of asynchronous communication.

blog (Weblog) A Web site that functions as an online journal or diary. One or more writers can post individual messages to the site, but writers cannot edit other users' posts.

course platform Software (such as Blackboard, CompClass, Desire2Learn, eCollege, or Moodle) that your college uses to host course content. A course platform might also be called *courseware, a course management system (CMS), a learning management system (LMS), or a virtual learning environment (VLE).*

download To save an online document (such as a handout from your course Web site) to your computer. Note that opening a document online doesn't automatically download it to your computer. For some assignments, your instructor might require that you download a form before you type on it.

post (verb) To type a comment or message online (*Be sure to post any peer comments by 10 p.m. Wednesday, April 13*). (noun) An online comment or message (*Your post about Kara's use of evidence was very smart.*)

synchronous Occurring at the same time or in real time. When students participate in synchronous discussions, they are all logged on to the course at the same time, and they can see (or hear) one another's comments in real time. Instant messaging is a form of synchronous communication.

upload To save a document (such as an essay) online, to the course Web site, for example. You will need to upload your assignments to the course Web site so that your instructor or peers (or both) can read them.

wiki A collaborative Web site that can be edited by many users. In writing classes, wikis are often used for group projects. One person might write a draft or section, and others will add to or edit the original text.

Index